JUL   2009

W9-CJD-132

A Robbie Reader

Meet Our New Student From

KOREA

Marylou Morano Kjelle

Mitchell Lane
PUBLISHERS

P.O. Box 196
Hockessin, Delaware 19707
Visit us on the web: www.mitchelllane.com
Comments? email us: mitchelllane@mitchelllane.com

Meet Our New Student From

Australia • China • Colombia • Great Britain
• Haiti • Israel • **Korea** • Malaysia • Mexico
• New Zealand • Nigeria • Tanzania

Copyright © 2009 by Mitchell Lane Publishers

Printing   1   2   3   4   5   6   7   8   9

PUBLISHER'S NOTE: The facts on which the story
in this book is based have been thoroughly
researched. Documentation of such research
can be found on page 45. While every possible
effort has been made to ensure accuracy, the
publisher will not assume liability for damages
caused by inaccuracies in the data, and
makes no warranty on the accuracy of the
information contained herein.

To reflect current usage, we have chosen to
use the secular era designations BCE
("before the common era") and CE ("of the
common era") instead of the traditional
designations BC ("before Christ") and AD
(*anno Domini*, "in the year of the Lord").

**Library of Congress Cataloging-in-Publication
Data**
Kjelle, Marylou Morano.
Meet our new student from Korea / by Marylou
Morano Kjelle.
   p. cm.
   Includes bibliographical references and index.
   ISBN 978-1-58415-649-9 (library bound)
1. Korea—Civilization—Juvenile literature.
I. Title.
   DS904.K5822 2009
   951.9—dc22

                                                    2008002276

                                                    PLB

CONTENTS

The United States celebrates Asian-American Heritage Month each May. During this time, Asian-Americans celebrate both their Asian heritage and their United States citizenship. These Korean girls, who live in the United States, watch a parade dressed in hanbok.

A Day to Learn
about Korea

Chapter

"Okay, class. It's time to settle down." Mrs. Williams, the third-grade teacher, spoke loudly to be heard over the classroom chatter.

It was the Monday after the Thanksgiving break, and Zach Parker, for once, was excited to be back in the Benjamin Franklin School in Bayville, New Jersey. Over the break, he and some of the other students had heard a bit of interesting news. A Korean family with a young boy had moved into the neighborhood. The boy was eight years old—just the right age to be in their class.

"Is it true, Mrs. Williams? Will the new boy from Korea be joining our class?" asked Zach.

"Yes," said Mrs. Williams. "Choi Kyung Hee will be joining our class tomorrow."

"Choi Kyung Hee? Is that his first name or his whole name?" asked Jessica Tate.

CHINA

Amnok (Yalu) River

Sinuiju

Nangnim Mountains

Hamgyong Mountains

Hyesan

Kanggye

Kimch'aek

Sonbon

Najin

Ch'ongjon

PYONGYANG

Namp'o

NORTH KOREA

Haeju

Wonsan

Kosang

DMZ

SEOUL

Inch'on

Suwon

Han River

EAST SEA (SEA OF JAPAN)

Mount Sorak National Park

Toebaek Mountains

Kangung

Tonghae

SOUTH KOREA

YELLOW SEA

Taejon

Chonju

Kwangju

Mokp'o

Yosu

Taegu

Masan

P'ohang

Ulsan

Pusan

JAPA

Where in the World

Demilitarized Zone

Korea Strait

Island of Cheju

▲ Halla-San

FACTS ABOUT SOUTH KOREA

Total area 38,022 square miles (98,480 square kilometers)

Population: 49,232,844 (July 2008 est.)

Capital: Seoul

Religions: Christianity, Buddhism

Languages: Korean, English widely taught in secondary school

Chief Exports: Semiconductors, wireless telecommunications equipment, motor vehicles, computers, steel, ships, petrochemicals

Monetary Unit: South Korean won

"*Choi* is Kyung Hee's last name," said Samantha Lantam. "Korean people give their last name first when they say their name. We would call him Kyung Hee Choi."

Samantha knew a lot about Korea. She had even been there. Two years before, her parents had adopted a baby girl named Soon from a Korean **orphanage** (OR-fuh-nidj). Samantha had traveled with her parents to pick up her new sister and bring her home to the United States.

"So in Korea," said Jessica, "I would be Tate Jessica!"

In the back of the classroom, Kyle Johnson raised his hand. "Mrs. Williams," he said, "I've never even heard of Korea. Where is it?"

"Samantha," asked Mrs. Williams, "would you please show the class where to find Korea on the world map?"

The entire class gathered around the large map hanging on the wall behind Mrs. Williams's desk. Samantha pointed to the continent of Asia, where Korea is located. "Korea is surrounded by water on three sides," she said. "It's a **peninsula**."

Figures she'd use a big word like that, Zach thought grouchily.

"What is this line running across the peninsula?" asked Ryan Kelly. "It looks like it's cutting Korea in half."

Chapter 1

Rock climbing is a favorite activity of South Koreans. The 800-foot-high Insu Peak at Pukhansan National Park, near Seoul, draws many rock climbers on the weekends.

"The Korean peninsula is divided into two separate countries, North Korea and South Korea. Although they are neighbors, they are very different," said Mrs. Williams. "Kyung Hee comes from South Korea." She asked the class to name the countries surrounding it.

"China is to the north of the Korean peninsula," said Kyle. "Russia is also close to North Korea."

"Good," said Mrs. Williams. "Now let's look at South Korea."

"The only country that touches it is North Korea," said Zach. He found himself getting interested anyway.

"Right," said Samantha. "The Yellow Sea is to the west of South Korea.""It is sometimes called the West Sea or the Korean Bay. It separates South Korea from China."

"The Korea Strait is south of the peninsula," said Jessica. "It separates South Korea from Japan."

"And the East Sea is to the east of South Korea," said Ryan.

Mrs. Williams said, "The East Sea is also known as the Sea of Japan. It also separates South Korea from Japan."

"What language does Kyung Hee speak?" asked Zach.

"What kind of food does he eat?" asked Jessica.

"Does he go to school?" asked Kyle.

There was a lot to learn about the new student who would soon be joining the class. And there was much to learn about Korea.

Ryan had an idea. "Mrs. Williams," he asked, "instead of doing our regular schoolwork, could we spend the whole day learning about Korea?"

"Could we? Please?" the other students asked.

Each part of the South Korean flag symbolizes something important to its people. The white stands for peace, and the red and blue represent the good and bad elements in the universe. These colors come together in a circle to show balance. The black symbols in each corner of the flag are called kwae. They stand for fire, earth, heaven, and water.

Cars are rare in Seoul, the capital of South Korea, and most people commute to and from the city on bicycles. When traveling by bike is not possible, commuters can also ride a cable car to get them where they need to go.

"It would be nice to learn as much as we can about Korea before Kyung Hee arrives," said Mrs. Williams. "Samantha, since you have been there, will you help us learn about Korea?"

"Sure," said Samantha. "Today is our day to learn about Korea."

That Samantha, thought Zach, *is such a smarty pants*. But he was glad he wouldn't be clueless when the new student arrived.

Korea

Many of the pavilions, shrines, and temples of South Korea have graceful, sloping roofs and wide columns. The style represents peace and harmony and an openness to nature.

"Land of the Morning Calm"

Chapter

People have lived on Korean land since **prehistoric** times. These early peoples probably came from the nearby countries of Russia, China, Mongolia, and Japan. They hunted wild animals and caught fish for food. Evidence shows they lived in the many caves found throughout the peninsula.

There is a **legend** that tells how Korea was founded. Around 2333 BCE, a leader named Dan-gun (whose name is sometimes spelled Tan'gun) became Korea's first king. According to the story, Dan-gun's father was a god and his mother was a woman who had once been a bear. Dan-gun united all the ancient peoples into one kingdom. He called this kingdom *Choson*, which means "land of the morning calm."

Dan-gun's descendants ruled Korea for more than one thousand years. Then Korea was divided into three major kingdoms: Silla, Koguryo, and Paekche.

Nature has a special place in the hearts of South Koreans, and Buddhist temples, such as this one, are usually constructed near water and mountains. Detailed designs, as seen on the bridge leading to the temple, are also common.

All three were influenced by China. By 372 CE, a religion from China, called Buddhism, was brought into Korea. Over time, Japan, China, Mongolia, and Russia each invaded Korea and tried to control its people. In 1910, Japan made Korea its **colony**.

Japan ruled Korea harshly until 1945, when World War II ended. Japan lost the war, and it had to give Korea **independence**. The United States and the Soviet Union were two governments that had fought against Japan. They agreed to work together to help Korea recover from Japanese rule. To do this, the Korean peninsula was divided in half. The Soviet Union, which was a **communist** country, took control of the northern part, and the United States, a **republic**, took control of the south. At the time, both governments hoped that Korea would one day be reunited and govern itself.

But Korea did not unite. In 1948, the leaders in the north formed a new country. They called it the Democratic People's Republic of Korea. Like the Soviet Union, North Korea became a communist country. Kim Il Sung, a respected leader in the north, took over as a dictator.

The United States helped South Korea become a free and independent country. It became known as the Republic of Korea. Like the United States, South Korea became a **democracy**. In 1948, Syngman Rhee was elected South Korea's first president.

Chapter 2

The two Koreas still did not live in peace. In 1950, armies from North Korea, with help from China, invaded South Korea, and tried to take it by force. The United States and other countries sent troops to help the South Koreans fight the North Koreans. The War between North and South Korea became known as the Korean War. It continued until 1953.

fun FACTS

North Korea is a little smaller than the state of Mississippi. South Korea is about the size of Indiana.

Although the fighting ended, Korea remained a divided country. A piece of land about 2.5 miles wide divided the two countries. This border is called the Demilitarized (dee-MIL-ih-tuh-ryzd) Zone, or DMZ. Soldiers from both countries patrol the DMZ night and day. The DMZ is the line on the map that divides North Korea from South Korea.

The communist government in North Korea rules its people harshly, and the North Korean people have few freedoms. Their government keeps them isolated (I-soh-lay-ted) from the rest of the world. It does not want people from other countries to visit. North Koreans are not allowed to leave their country, but some secretly cross into China. If they return, they are arrested. Many of these **refugees** (REH-fyoo-jees) make their way to the United States, where they settle. The United States does not approve of the way North Korea treats its people. The governments of North Korea and the United States are not on friendly terms.

On the other hand, South Korean citizens enjoy the same freedoms that Americans do. The United States and South Korea are friendly. Each year many South Koreans visit the United States. Some stay for a long time. Others make the United States their home.

In Seoul, a South Korean war veteran proudly wears his uniform more than fifty years after the end of the Korean War. Over 227,000 South Koreans died in the war, and more than 717,000 were wounded.

To symbolize their work toward bringing the two Koreas together, the leaders of both countries planted a tree with soil taken from both countries. This ceremony took place in Pyongyang, North Korea, on October 4, 2007.

In 2007, the presidents of both North Korea and South Korea met to discuss bringing their two countries together. At the end of the meeting, South Korean president Roh Moo-hyun (left) shook hands with North Korean leader Kim Jong Il.

There is hope that one day North Korea and South Korea will work closer together. In 2007, the leaders of both countries held a meeting. They talked about eight ways to bring the two Koreas together. It will take a lot of time and hard work. Still, a start has been made, and that may be good not only for the Korean people, but for all people.

Korea

South Koreans like to vacation on Cheju Island, which they call the Island of the Gods. Swimming, fishing, golfing, horseback riding, and mountain climbing are some of the things to do there. People who have visited both Cheju and the United States' Hawaiian Islands say they are quite alike.

A Mountainous Peninsula

Chapter 3

Thousands of islands lie to the south and west of South Korea. They are really underwater mountains whose peaks rise out of the water. The west coast of the Korean peninsula is mostly plains, but rugged mountains cover much of both North Korea and South Korea. The Hamgyong and Nangnim mountain ranges are found in the northeast section of North Korea.

The largest mountain range in South Korea is the Taebaek Mountains along the East Coast. The highest peak in South Korea is Halla-san, which is almost 6,400 feet high. Halla-san is an **extinct** volcano that forms the island of Cheju, which lies to the south of South Korea's mainland.

Tourists are welcome in South Korea, and many visit Sorak-san National Park in the northern part of the country. There they hike and view beautiful scenery, including waterfalls. Other fun things to do

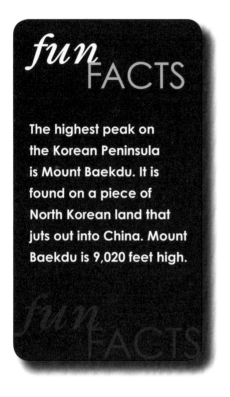

*fun*FACTS

The highest peak on the Korean Peninsula is Mount Baekdu. It is found on a piece of North Korean land that juts out into China. Mount Baekdu is 9,020 feet high.

in the mountains of South Korea include skiing, rock climbing, and camping.

The forests of Korea are filled with maple, pine, and elm trees. Weasels, deer, wild boars, rabbits, squirrels, and red foxes live in the forests, as do larger mammals, such as the Siberian tiger, black bear, and lynx. Many of the larger mammals are **endangered** because people cut down the forests and build houses there, and because of hunting. The black-billed magpie, hawks, pheasants (FEH-zents), and woodpeckers also make their homes in the mountainous forests.

Many wide and deep rivers flow down from the Korean mountains and empty into the Yellow Sea. Korea's rivers are used for transportation and **irrigation** (eer-ih-GAY-shun). The longest river in North Korea is the Amnok, or Yalu, which is about 500 miles long. It separates North Korea from China. The two longest rivers in South Korea are the Han and the Naktong. They are each about 300 miles long.

The Siberian tiger is the largest of the tiger species, weighing about 600 pounds. Wildlife experts fear there may be fewer than 500 Siberian tigers living in the wild. Many more are cared for humanely in zoos and circuses.

Rice is the main crop of South Korea. Farmers grow rice in paddies and use the rivers to water them. Other crops grown in South Korea are watermelon, barley, red peppers, and Chinese cabbage. Apples, pears, peaches, and tangerines are also grown there. Many families keep small gardens for growing some of the food they eat.

Spicy red peppers dry in the sun. Korean food is known for its spicy flavor, which is added by using ingredients such as onions, ginger, garlic, and red peppers.

The Korean magpie is the national bird of South Korea.

Lakes and caves are also found throughout Korea. Underground natural resources include lead, graphite, tungsten, and coal. Some of these resources are used to produce goods that are shipped to other parts of the world. These products include wireless communication equipment, cars, and ships.

The Korean peninsula has four seasons, and strong winds blow across the land all year long. The winter winds blow down from a cold part of Russia called

The rose of Sharon is the national flower of South Korea.

One or two typhoons hit the Korean Peninsula each summer. In September 2007, Typhoon Nari hit Cheju Island, killing at least 14 people.

Siberia. The winds bring with them extremely cold temperatures—as low as 15°F. Spring winds sweep in from Asia, and summer winds, called monsoons, bring heavy rains. Typhoons—large storms with strong winds and heavy rains—occur every few years in Korea. In September 2003, Typhoon Maemi, the strongest typhoon in 100 years, slammed into South Korea and killed at least 85 people.

Korea

The city of Pusan, also known as Busan, is South Korea's second largest city (after Seoul) and its largest harbor. One of Pusan's major tourist attractions is the Pusan Tower, which was built in 1973 and is 120 meters (almost 400 feet) tall. Visitors can take in many spectacular views of the city and the water from the tower.

People of
Tradition

Chapter

Koreans live both on farms and in cities, but most Koreans live in cities because more jobs are there. Many people work in manufacturing. They make clothing, **appliances** (ah-PLY-unt-ses), metal, computers, and ships.

About 49 million people live in South Korea. Seoul, the capital, has 11 million people living there. With so many people living in one city, the easiest way to get around is by bicycle. It is a modern city with lively outdoor markets.

Unlike the United States, which is a **melting pot**, most of the people who live in Korea were born there. Few foreigners live in their country. Religion is discouraged in North Korea because it is a communist society, but religion is important to the South Koreans. There, people practice Buddhism, a religion that follows the teachings of Gautama Buddha, a spiritual guide from ancient India. South Koreans also practice Confucianism (kun-FYOO-shun-ism), the way of thinking of Confucius, a teacher who lived in China in ancient times. Some South Koreans are Christians.

One of the most popular holidays in Korea is Children's Day. It is celebrated each year on May 5. On this day, families spend time together. Parents usually take their kids to public places such as an amusement park or a zoo.

Foundation Day, on October 3, celebrates the founding of the *Choson* kingdom in 2333 BCE. Korean families celebrate by gathering together in

At the War Museum in Seoul, a special forces soldier from the South Korean army breaks stone plates with his bare hands at a Children's Day event.

South Korean children watch a martial arts contest as part of a National Foundation Day celebration at the Korean Folk Museum in Seoul. Other ways Koreans celebrate National Foundation Day are with parades and ceremonies.

one another's homes or by eating out in restaurants. In Pyongyang, North Korea, special ceremonies are held at the burial place of Korea's founder, Dan-gun. Wine is offered to his soul, and a moment of silence is offered in his memory.

A Korean holiday like Thanksgiving in the United States is Chuseok, or Harvest Moon Festival. This three-day holiday occurs after the harvest. Korean families celebrate Chuseok by visiting the birthplace of their

ancestors. They eat special foods made from the fruits and vegetables they have harvested. They also eat *songpyeon*, a dough made from rice powder that has been stuffed with red beans, chestnuts, and sesame seeds and then steamed.

For work, school, or play, Koreans wear the same type of clothing that Americans wear. But for special occasions, such as Chuseok and weddings, Koreans wear traditional dress called *hanbok*. Women wear

Although simple in design, traditional Korean dress is dazzling in color. *Hanbok* was once worn every day, but now it is worn only for weddings and other special occasions.

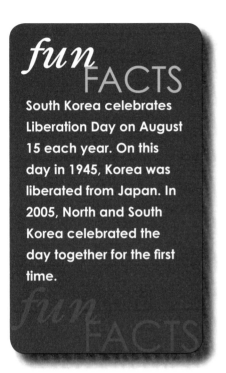

colorful skirts called *chima* with short jackets or blouses called *jeogori* (sometimes spelled *chogari*). When wearing a *hanbok*, women place ribbons in their hair and carry colorful fans. The *hanbok* worn by men is a *jeogori* with a *paji*—loose-fitting pants gathered at the ankles. Wearing traditional dress shows respect, especially to the older members of the family. Another way people show respect to one another is by bowing when they meet.

Korean students go to elementary, middle, and high school. They study science, math, and social studies, just like American children do. Korean is the main language of both North and South Korea, but when they get to high school, South Korean students study English and other languages, such as French and German. Few North Korean students learn languages other than Korean. Many South Korean students go to college.

Korean children like to play soccer, and they play a Korean chess game called *changgi*. Making and

Fish is one of the most popular foods in Korea, and because the country is a peninsula, seafood is abundant. Grains, rice, and vegetables also make up the Korean diet.

The average Korean eats about 40 pounds of *kimchi* each year.

flying kites is another way Korean children have fun. They also practice tae kwon do (ty kwon DOH), a form of **martial arts** that is like karate.

Koreans eat a lot of vegetables, fruit, and fish. They also eat beef and chicken. Their food is very spicy. Rice is served at every meal, and food is eaten with chopsticks. *Kimchi* is one of the most popular foods in Korea. It is made by **fermenting** a vegetable such as cabbage, radish, or cucumber and adding spices to it. *Kimchi* may be eaten at every meal.

Korea

Like every major capital city, Seoul offers residents and visitors bright lights and exciting things to do after the sun goes down.

An Nyong Ha Seyo, Kyung Hee!

Chapter 5

"I have an idea," said Mrs. Williams near the end of the day. "Why don't we show Kyung Hee how much we know about Korea by having a party in his honor."

The students put their heads together and came up with a plan. They would decorate their classroom to welcome their new classmate. They would also prepare a Korean snack to share with him. And since they had art class on Tuesdays, the students decided they would make kites for that week's art project.

The next morning, Zach, Samantha, and the other students were in their classroom bright and early. It was Kyung Hee's first day, and they wanted to welcome him in a special way.

While Samantha hung a sign on the door that said, "Welcome, Kyung Hee," Zach placed small South Korean flags around the room. Kyle placed the paper, sticks, and string needed to make the kites on the table in the back of the classroom. And Ryan and

Jessica put out the Korean snack the children had chosen: raw vegetables and a sesame seed sauce for dipping called *cho kanjang* (choh KAN-chung).

Soon a boy with straight black hair peeked into the room. "Is this Mrs. Williams's classroom?" he asked.

"*An nyong ha seyo! An nyong ha seyo!*" the children said, and bowed to their new classmate. "Hello! Hello!"

"*An nyong ha seyo!*" he replied, bowing back. "I am Kyung Hee, but I have chosen an American name. Please call me Paul."

"Welcome, Paul," said Mrs. Williams.

"*Kamsa hamnida,*" said Paul. "Thank you."

The students were eager to get to know Paul and to learn about his life in Korea. Paul told his new classmates that his father was a research scientist who had gotten a job at the state university. And Paul's father, mother, and older sister, Mi-sook, had just bought their first car.

"In Korea we lived in Seoul, the capital," said Paul. "There we rode bikes because there was no other way to get around. Here in the United States, kids ride their bikes for fun."

"Hey, do you want to go bike riding after school?" asked Zach. "We can ride to the park near my house. There's a baseball and soccer field there, too."

"Sure!" said Paul. "But I'm not very good at baseball."

"I can teach you," said Zach. "My dad's the coach for our team."

Linda Sue Park
Linda Sue Park was born in Illinois on March 25, 1960. Her parents moved from Korea to the United States before Linda Sue was born. She grew up near Chicago. When she was four years old, she started writing poetry. As an adult, she wrote many books for children that take place in Korea. Her first novel, *Seesaw Girl*, takes place in Korea in the 1600s. In 2001, she released *A Single Shard*, a novel about a Korean named Tree-ear who lives in the 1100s. This book won a Newbery Medal, one of the highest awards a children's book can receive. Linda Sue lives with her family in New York.

Paul and his sister hang out at their school in Seoul. Education is taken seriously in South Korea. After a full day in the classroom, students work for several hours each evening on their homework. Private schools and many public schools require students to wear uniforms to school.

Paul had many questions to ask his new friends about America. They spent the whole day getting to know one another. They spoke of the children's book author Linda Sue Park, whose parents were born in Korea. They ate the vegetables dipped in sesame seed sauce, and they made kites and hung them around the room.

Paul was amazed by how much the students knew about his native home. And the students in his class were very happy to welcome their new student from Korea.

Sesame Seed Sauce
(Cho Kanjang)

This recipe can also be served with hot vegetables or as a sauce for meat.

Instructions

Ask an adult to help you make this recipe.

1. **With the help of an adult**, toast the sesame seeds in a dry frying pan over medium heat for about 5 minutes or until they start to turn the color of toast. Keep stirring so that they don't burn.
2. Place the toasted sesame seeds in a blender and crush them.
3. Scrape the crushed sesame seeds into a bowl. Add the sugar, vinegar, and soy sauce. Stir to mix well.
4. Serve with vegetables for dipping.

Things You Will Need

An adult
Frying pan
Stove
Wooden spoon
Blender
Bowl
Measuring cup
Tablespoon

Ingredients

½ cup sesame seeds
1 tablespoon sugar
3 tablespoons vinegar
4 tablespoons light soy sauce
Vegetables for dipping (such as baby carrots, broccoli pieces, and cucumber spears)

Make Your Own
Decorative Kite

You Will Need

Construction Paper

Glue

Colored String

Glitter

Beads

Ribbon to Make Bows

Kites play an important role in Korean folklore. One legend says that in the seventh century, a Korean general used a kite with a fireball attached to it to inspire his troops to conquer an enemy. Today in Korea, kites are flown on holidays by both kids and adults, and kite fighting—where opponents try to knock each other's kites out of the sky—is a popular sport.

Instructions for Making Decorative Kite

1. Cut a piece of construction paper so that it is 10 inches square. Save the long strips that you cut off.

2. Position the square piece of paper so that it sits like a diamond. Glue the strips of construction paper across and down, from corner to corner.

3. Use the ribbon to make 4 to 6 bows. Tie them to a piece of ribbon or string that is 1 to 2 feet long.

4. Glue the string to the bottom corner of the paper.

5. Decorate your kite with beads and glitter, or personalize it with your name.

Further Reading

Books

Behnke, Alison. *North Korea in Pictures*. Minneapolis: Lerner Publications, 2005.

———. *South Korea in Pictures*. Minneapolis: Lerner Publications, 2005.

Chung, Okwha, and Judy Monroe. *Cooking the Korean Way*. Minneapolis: Lerner Publications, 2003.

De Capua, Sarah. *Korea: Discovering Cultures*. Tarrytown, New York: Benchmark Books, 2005.

Feldman, Ruth Tenzer. *The Korean War*. Chronicle of American Wars. Minneapolis: Lerner Publications, 2004.

Haberle, Susan E. *North Korea: A Question and Answer Book*. Mankato, Minnesota: Capstone Press, 2005.

———. South Korea: *A Question and Answer Book*. Mankato, Minnesota: Capstone Press, 2005.

Park, Frances, and Ginger Park. *My Freedom Trip: A Child's Escape from North Korea*. Honesdale, Pennsylvania: Boyds Mill Press, 1998.

On the Internet

Connor, Mary. Famous Koreans: Six Portraits
http://www.aasianst.org/EAA/connor.htm

"The Fighter Kites of Korea"
http://www.drachen.org/pdf/Student-Readings/
FighterKitesofKorea.pdf

The Korean War Website
http://www.korean-war.com/

Linda Sue Park, Official Website
http://www.lspark.com

The Republic of Korea Official Website
http://www.korea.net/

Works Consulted

The author consulted with many Korean friends and neighbors for the information in this book. Other sources are listed below.

Clark, Donald N. *Culture and Customs of Korea*. Westport, Connecticut: Greenwood Press, 2000.

Cummings, Bruce. *Korea's Place in the Sun*. New York: W.W. Norton & Company, 1997.

Hoare, James. *Korea Culture Smart*. Portland, Oregon: Graphic Arts Center Publishing Company, 2005.

Ki-baik Lee. *A New History of Korea*. Translated by Edward W. Wagner with Edward J. Shultz. Seoul: Ilchokak Publishers, 1984.

"Korean Leaders Sign Peace Pledge." *CNN*, October 5, 2007. http://www.cnn.com/2007/WORLD/asiapcf/10/04/koreas. summit/index.html

Library of Congress, Federal Research Division. Country Studies: South Korea. Accessed September 1, 2007. http://lcweb2.loc.gov/frd/cs/krtoc.html

"Sesame Seed Sauce Recipe" Asian Online Recipes. Accessed September 9, 2007. http://www.asianonlinerecipes.com/ online_recipes/korea/sesame-seed-sauce.php

Vegdahl, Sonja, and Ben Seunghwa Hur. *Korea*. CultureShock! Portland, Oregon: Graphic Arts Center Publishing Company, 2005.

Yoo, Yushin. *Korea the Beautiful: Treasures of the Hermit Kingdom*. Los Angeles: The Golden Pond Press, 1987.

Embassy

The Republic of Korea
2450 Massachusetts Avenue, NW
Washington, DC 20008
Telephone: (202) 939-5600
URL: http://www.koreaembassyusa.org/

Glossary

appliances (ah-PLY-unt-ses)—Large machines used in the home, such as the refrigerator, washer, and dryer.

colony (KAH-luh-nee)—A country or state that is ruled by another country or state.

communist (KOM-yoo-nist)—A type of government in which everything is owned by the government and individual citizens own nothing.

democracy (deh-MAH-kruh-see)—A form of government in which the people vote for their leaders.

endangered (en-DAYN-jerd)—Threatened with extinction.

extinct (ek-STINKT)—No longer active or living.

fermenting (fer-MEN-ting)—Going through a chemical change that causes bubbles of gas to form.

independence (in-dee-PEN-dents)—The freedom to rule or take care of oneself.

irrigation (eer-ih-GAY-shun)—A system for watering crops.

legend (LEH-jend)—A story that seems unreal and cannot be proven, yet has been told for many generations.

martial art (MAR-shul ARTS)—A type of self-defense or style of combat that many people practice for sport (such as karate).

melting pot (MEL-ting pot)—A society made up of people who come from many different races and cultures.

orphanage (OR-fuh-nidj)—A place that cares for children who no longer have parents.

peninsula (peh-NIN-suh-luh)—A narrow strip of land that is almost completely surrounded by water.

prehistoric (pree-his-TOR-ik)—The time before history was recorded in writing.

refugees (REH-fyoo-jees)—A group of people who leave one country or area to find safety in another.

republic (ree-PUB-lik)—A form of government in which the people vote for their representatives. A democracy.

Index

ABOUT THE AUTHOR

Marylou Morano Kjelle lives and works in a central New Jersey community where more than 30 percent of the residents have an Asian heritage. Even the mayor of her town is Korean-American. At Rutgers University, where she teaches writing, Marylou has many Korean-born and Korean-American students. Some of the information for this book came from her students and neighbors.

Marylou is the author of dozens of children's books, including *A Kid's Guide to Landscape Design*, *Dwayne "The Rock" Johnson*, and *What's So Great About Jacques Cartier?* for Mitchell Lane Publishers. When she is not teaching or writing books for young readers, she works as a reporter for a local newspaper.